The Simple Tax System

The Simple Tax System
Replacing the U.S. Tax Code with a Revolutionary Simple Tax System

by

Daniel V. Carbaugh, BA, MS

Copyright © 2024 by Daniel V. Carbaugh.

All rights reserved. No part of this publication may be reproduced, distributed, or transmitted in any form or by any means, including photocopying, recording, or other electronic or mechanical methods, without the prior written permission of the copyright owner and the publisher, except in the case of brief quotations embodied in critical reviews and certain other noncommercial uses permitted by copyright law. For permission requests, write to the publisher, addressed "Attention: Permissions Coordinator," at the address below.

CITIOFBOOKS, INC.
3736 Eubank NE Suite A1
Albuquerque, NM 87111-3579
www.citiofbooks.com
Hotline: 1 (877) 389-2759
Fax: 1 (505) 930-7244

Ordering Information:
Quantity sales. Special discounts are available on quantity purchases by corporations, associations, and others. For details, contact the publisher at the address above.

Printed in the United States of America.

ISBN-13:	Softcover	979-8-89391-095-7
	eBook	979-8-89391-096-4

Library of Congress Control Number: 2024908962

Contents

The Sample Tax System i
Foreword 1
About the Book 3
Introducing the Simple Tax System 5
The Simple Tax System Presentation 8
Ramblings 48
Damn the U.S. Tax Code 52
Reform 53
How It Works 59
Congress - A Player 62
Consumers and Benefactors 64
Money for Nothing 66
The Author - Out of Control 68
Good People and Questions 72
All for One... One for All. 74
Dollars and Sense 76
And...? 77

Foreword

"We might be better off if we replaced every member of Congress with a random selection of individuals from the 'White Pages." Anonymous

Not too long after I retired, I discovered that I had a lot of free time on my hands, free time I hadn't planned on. I tried several mundane activities to fill the void, long bicycle rides, all day golf outings with buddies, excursions to the cinema.

Often my daily routine included a visit to the community pool, another time-killing activity. Usually this exercise started reluctantly, but after getting accustomed to the wet environment it quickly became a peaceful, relaxing daily experience.

Such as an abundance of free time would dictate, I had the leisure, in and out of the pool, to ponder many important issues of the day, like, did I remember to restock my beer supply for the weekend? Which movie should I put on my must-watch list for tomorrow? Should we eat in or go out for dinner tonight? Nothing really crucial but still important to a man with time on his hands.

Around late February of 2014, my monkey-mind began to focus on the 15th of April-Tax Day. Was I ready to begin the paperwork grind for my yearly tax return? Would I need an extension this year to file? Would I get audited? Several issues began to engage my mind and bother my daily routine, all dealing with the annual tax filing necessity.

Why am I intimidated by the IRS? Why do I fear this agency? Why is filing my tax return so stressful? They weren't new questions. I asked them last year too, ... and the year before... and the year before, etc. I knew these questions would continue to haunt me as long as the current tax system existed.

Every U.S. taxpayer knows that the IRS is powerful. It is a para-police organization.

The IRS can arrest you, take your wealth and possessions, and put you in jail. Fear and intimidation are certainly justified.

The federal government has several para-police organizations, but the IRS is the most notorious because it touches every citizen and legal resident, i.e., everyone who has an income or has the ability and authority to make an income. The IRS is universally despised by most all of *We the People*, even those of us who work at the agency.

Frankly, after 81 years on the planet, 57 years as a taxpayer, I've given up. I can no longer file my taxes without a lot of help and accompanied grief. I don't understand the jargon, the rules, the requirements and the confusing, meaningless directions. Without the aid of jazzy software prog rams, an accountant and a university professor of economics in my hip pocket, I can't adequately respond to anything past my name and address. And, after I finally file my once-a-year return. My summer months are ruined by fear of receiving that dreaded "We want to talk to you" letter from the IRS. Even when I put my tax return in the hands of professional bean-counters, I still fear an audit or other nefarious response from the IRS. I sometimes wonder if the protection and benefits given to me by the U.S. Government are worth it.

When Congress decides to reform taxes, it really means the U.S. Tax Code will become more voluminous and more confusing. Some forward thinkers have proposed alternatives to the complicated morass of directions in the code, i.e., a *National Sales Tax*, the *Flat Tax* and the *Fair Tax*. Any of these would be far better than the current system. But I argue that none of these change the culture in the IRS; they just make the process simpler for the individual, i.e., fewer documents, fewer directions. Then with time and passing administrations the code begins to grow again, until another reform is the politically expedient thing to do. Unfortunately, however, Congress chooses to talk about these alternatives, hold committee meetings on them, and opine in the media. They can't seem to bring themselves to implement just one of these alternatives as law. What they most often do not discuss is where the money comes from. They assume *income* is the only source.

Everyone who enjoys the protection and benefits from the U.S. Federal Government has an obligation to give of themselves toward the goal of paying for those protections and benefits. The current tax system, which most of us loathe, is riddled with one hundred years of special interests meddling for favors. The U.S. Tax Code is badly broken and far beyond repair. It has to be repealed and replaced (where have I heard that expression before?). But we have to be careful. It can't be scrapped all at once. Its demise has to be like building a house around an existing kitchen. We have to rebuild to new dimensions and think about novel and extraordinary solutions (outside the box).

Therefore, I am offering my own ideas for a new tax system that not only replaces the current system for taxpaying individuals but can also be applied to businesses small and large.

ABOUT THE BOOK

This body of work is an update to the first printing issued on 21 September 2015, titled Simple Tax Reform: The New201* Tax System. The name of the proposed tax system was changed to The Simple Tax System (STS). Subsequently, the title of the book was likewise changed to The Simple Tax System: Replacing the U.S. Tax Code with a Revolutionary Simple Tax System.

This later publication, as did the original, describes the framework for a new U.S. tax system- a tax system that affects the individual taxpayer and the business taxpayer. I call it the Simple Tax System because it's simple; it's about our collective obligation to fund the federal government, and from beginning to end it's a complete, indivisible system.

I believe that reform of the current tax system (the U.S. Tax Code), along the lines of changing tax brackets, eliminating loopholes, and tinkering with regulations, is not enough, even if it changes or eliminates the aggressive nature of the IRS.

So, I have crafted the The Simple Tax System (STS) to radically change the IRS mission and strip away most of its para-police posture and policies. If adopted, *We the People* will no longer fear the IRS.

Well then, if we will no longer fear the IRS after we change over to the Simple Tax System, then who will we fear?

The answer is, as it is, as it always has been...Congress, the President, and the Supreme Court.

As believers fear God the Almighty and Judgment Day, taxpayers will always fear those whom they are forced to sustain.

This book is organized as follows: The Foreword is followed by a PowerPoint presentation much like you would find in a business or classroom setting. If you've had enough after slogging through the presentation, good for you; you can stop then. At that point you'll have the information I want you to have. But I'm not going to let you off that easily. Following the PowerPoint presentation is a variety of explanations, opinions, and ramblings built around notes associated with each presentation page.

INTRODUCING THE SIMPLE TAX SYSTEM

The Simple Tax System (STS). Presented herein is flatter, fairer and more politically correct than anything that has a chance to replace the existing personal income tax system. Hang on! We'll get to it in a minute

Remember - Monikers are important.

When skimming through the various sections of this book, keep in mind that my focus is on the current tax system that provides funds for the operation of the federal government. I am proposing a new tax system that will generate the same funds as the system it's replacing- essentially the income tax and all its procedures and the tax on businesses. For now, it's enough to say that corporate taxes are far too high. History verifies when corporate taxes are low, the economy flourishes better than when corporate taxes are high. To deny history is to ignore logic. I believe one who denies history is simply stupid; not ignorant, just stupid. And it's tough to fix stupid.

A plethora of tax systems have been proposed to replace the cumbersome mess we currently use. If you care to bore yourself to tears, I suggest you google the ones that tickle your fancy. Novels have been written about the most popular alternatives. Listed here are a few of the most popular alternatives: Milton Friedman's Flat Tax, the Heritage Foundation's New Flat tax, Richard Woodsall's the Fair Tax, Hennan Cain's 999 Tax, Ben Carson's (and God's) Tithing and the general idea of a simple National Sales Tax.

After reading about them there's just one more to talk about: The Simple Tax System (STS). But since the center piece of the Simple Tax System (STS) is a National Sales Tax, let's explore the NST a little at this point.

A National Sales Tax is a rather simple approach for generating revenue; tax everything you buy with a flat tax. Opponents argue that low income earners are hit harder than middle and high income earners. I never could understand this argument since 10% of an income with no disposable income is equally stressed as is 10% of a middle or high income with no disposable income.

Note: I have purposely introduced the concept of "disposable income" to appease those who make the argument; the counter argument is that middle and high income earners most always have some level of disposable income; more on "disposable income" later.

The problem with a National Sales tax, like that proposed in the popular alternatives previously mentioned, is the sticker shock of the tax rate (17% to 29%). Those numbers are hard to swallow unless the taxpaying public can understand how the national sales tax rate will generate the same amount of funds (or more). That is to say, one has to be convinced that they will be paying the same amount or less, not more than with the present system. Personally, I can't understand why people are skeptical on this issue. It seems that we don't believe that our legislators are being truthful when they propose such a simple system that generates the same revenue as the complex one now in place. Taxpayers must think that efficiency and simplicity should generate more revenue ...or, that simplicity and efficiency will actually reduce expenditures, resulting in savings. What a misinformed lot they are! Huh? Insert Mutley here.

So, one of the questions is, "Would you agree to pay, say, 19% of your income to the federal government if the process was made so simple your pre-teen son could complete all the paper-work in 30 minutes?"

Why are we collecting taxes on incomes? Why don't we look at "out of the box" sources for funding the government? Why do the Feds ignore how forty-three states collect funds to pay for their essential services?

Forty-three states collect funds through the application of taxes on the sale of goods and services. Some states allow exemptions to their sales tax, items like basic food and clothing. That's good. Within today's technology (inventory control through the application of queried databases) any item can be tagged with flags that selectively apply different tax rates to different commodities. This is no longer a difficult task. It's really a piece of cake. Technology is so advanced that items can be tagged with any tax rate level. Categories of goods and services can be as complicated as our bureaucrat's desire to make them.

Exemptions could also be identified with a national sales tax. Knowing how bureaucrats complicate the simple, I can imagine they would assign a different tax rate to every item they want to tax.

But the central item of The Simple Tax System is a flat sales tax rate. Throughout the remainder of my explanation, I have decided to assign 12.5% as the central national sales tax. This rate would be coupled to the state sales tax rate in those forty-three states that have a state sales tax. So, Florida will tax all goods and services at 18.5% instead of 6%. The reason to piggy-back the national sales tax rate to the state sales tax rate is simple - the collection process and state sales tax bureaucracy already exists. This fact will facilitate the collection of the national sales tax in all but 7 states. We'll deal with those Dirty Seven later.

Each state will continue to collect sales taxes as before, however 12.5% of the taxes collected will be transferred to the IRS. The IRS still has collection responsibilities; however, they collect taxes from the states not the individual; this change is a BIGGIE!

Initially, the easiest way to deal with exemptions and different rates for special items would be apply the state's rules to the federal rules (after the feds deliberate on the tax rate and the exemption considerations). Essentially the Feds would require each state to continue their existing sales tax policy and procedures with a new rate (increased by the addition of the fed sales tax rate). Those seven states without a sales tax will have to ante up - should be an easy transition for them as they certainly have forty-three models to choose from.

So, to get the ball rolling each state has to sign up. Short of a mandate, each state has to agree to slightly modify their existing sales tax process to accommodate The Simple Tax System (STS). Nothing could be easier (tongue in cheek, huh)?

The Simple Tax System Presentation

THE SIMPLE TAX SYSTEM - A PROPOSAL

The following presentation outlines a framework of an alternative taxing \system that, if adopted by Congress, will radically reform the current US Tac Code for individual and businesses.

This new revenue generating system is hereafter referred to as:

The Simple Tax System

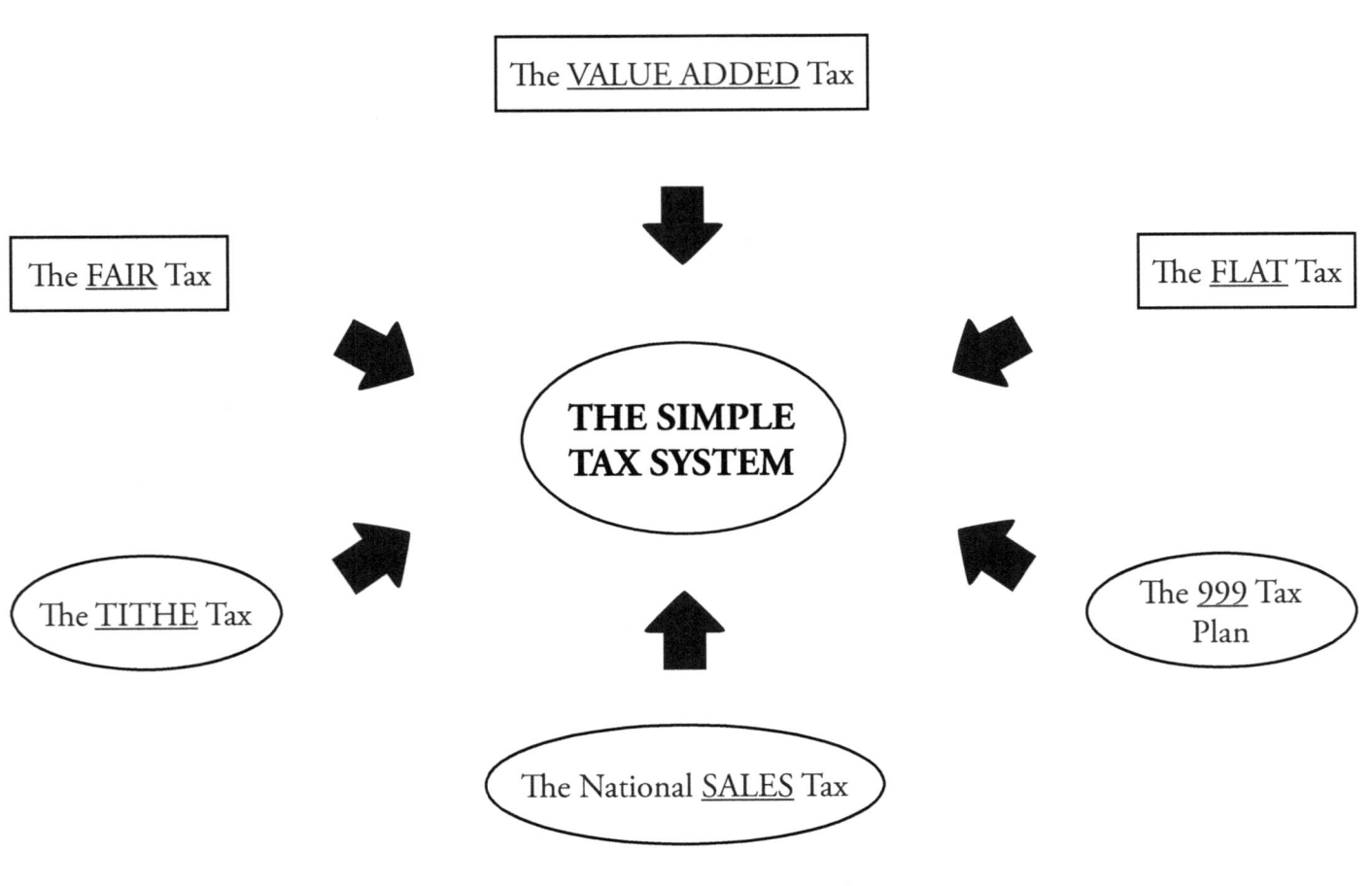

Figure 1-1 Alternative Tax Plans

The Simple Tax System
Another Tax Proposal – WHY?

The US Tax Code

- Too complicated – a gazillion pages (approx. 75,000)
- Not flat; not fair – too many brackets; top heavy
- Not relevant – no longer meaningful to American taxpayer
- Not manageable – the IRS doesn't understand it either
- COERCIVE – enforced by the IRS; fines, leans and jail time
- Pandered – Infiltrated by Special Interests (K St. lobbyists)

Why Do *"We the People"* Fear the IRS?

The IRS is a federal agency with POLICE-like powers. Concerning matters of <u>your</u> delinquent taxes, the IRS considers <u>you</u> GUILTY until you prove your innocence.

The IRS has the power to:

- *INTIMIDATE* you (make you feel like a criminal)
- *GARNISH* (steal) your WAGES
- SEIZE (steal) your PROPERTY ... even your HOME!
- Put LEINS on (steal) your ASSETS, and... generally

MAKE YOUR LIFE MESIRABLE!

The Simple Tax System, ... Going In ...

Any proposal must consider the objections of the political left and the right.

The left wants to take care of minorities and punish the worthy. They like a progressive bracket system; high earners paying more.

The right wants a system that treats everyone the same and is simple to obey; a system with incentives to stop dependence on government.

Also, the scraping of the old and implementing the new must be easy and quick. Existing agencies and complementary businesses must welcome the changes as merely a shift in missions not a radical destruction of them.

The new system must take advantage of existing state and federal bureaucracies, in-place processes and procedures. There must be the perception that government is going to be somewhat smaller as a result of the upcoming reforms.

The Simple Tax System

> Above all else, The Simple Tax System (STS) must be perceived as non-corruptible, and a FAIR and efficient method to fund the essential tasks of the Federal government.

<u>Main Features of The Simple Tax System:</u>

- Totally scrapes the individual income tax system as it is now exists.
  - ***Taxes are now derived from purchases, not income***

- Shifts enforcement authority from the IRS to the States
  - ***A new image for the IRS – a bigger role for the States***

- Adds a yearly assessment fee to high income earners.
  - ***Success fosters financial gratitude on continuing income gains.***

- Provide lower income earners incentive to become successful.
  - ***Allows for significant rebates of taxes paid.***

- All citizens and legal residents will participate (pay taxes)
  - ***Everyone will have some "skin in the game"***

- Eliminates the need for Federal Withholding Tax
  - ***Provides a monthly stream of money to the US Treasury***

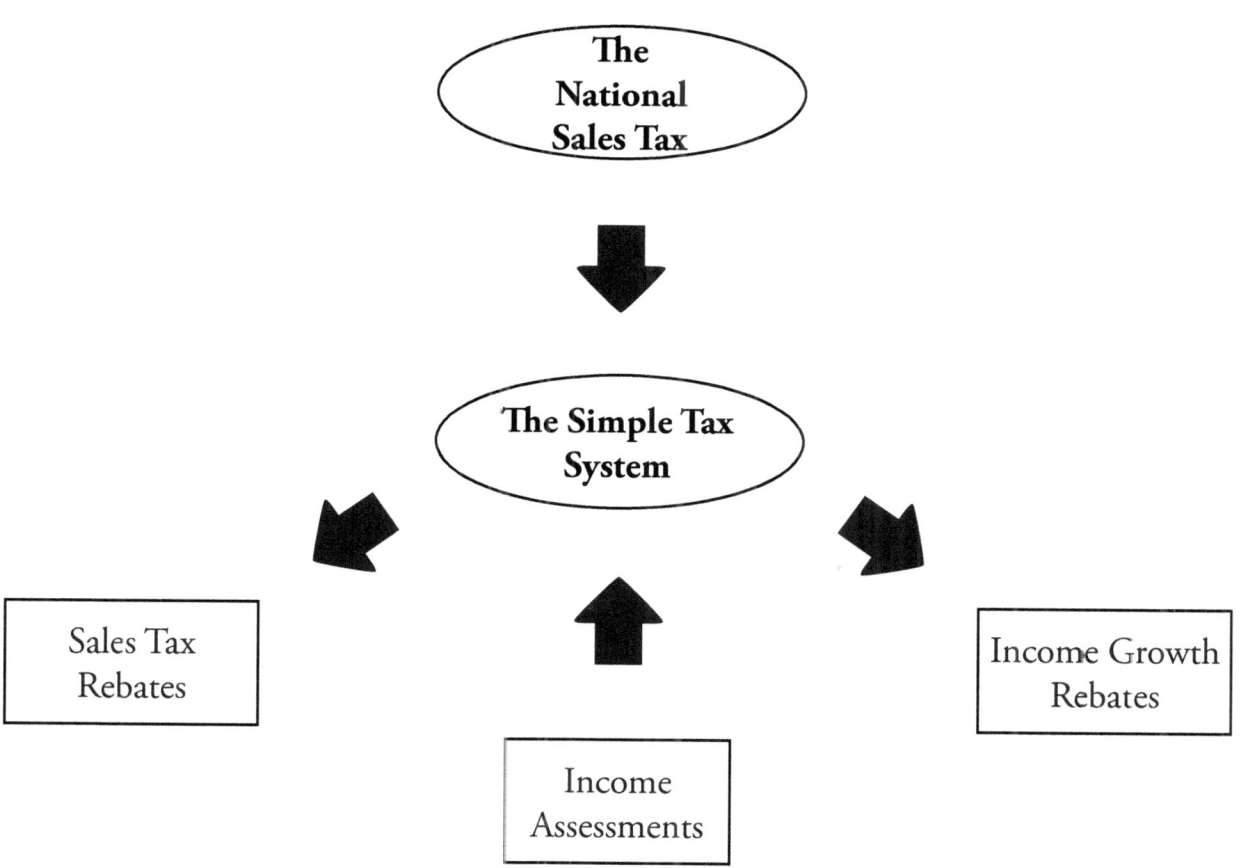

Figure 1-2 The Simple Tax System

A New Image for the IRS
What will the IRS do and not do?

The IRS **will**, for the moment, remain as the collector of tax receipts for the US treasury.

The IRS **will** continue to collect income information, verify and acknowledge the income of citizens, legal residents and guest's workers.

The IRS **will** provide the States with verified individual profile (initially only on high income earners).

The IRS **will** issue rebates to taxpayers and tax vouchers to Special People.

The IRS **will** collect monthly tax receipts and yearly assessment receipts and forward these funds to the US Treasury.

The IRS **will** establish a Tax Liaison Agency with the States. Etc., *to ensure compliance with The Simple Tax System (STS) law

Note 1: The IRS will no longer collect funds directly from taxpayers.
Note 2: *The abbreviation, Etc., refers to the US Territories and other places where citizens and legal residents can vote.

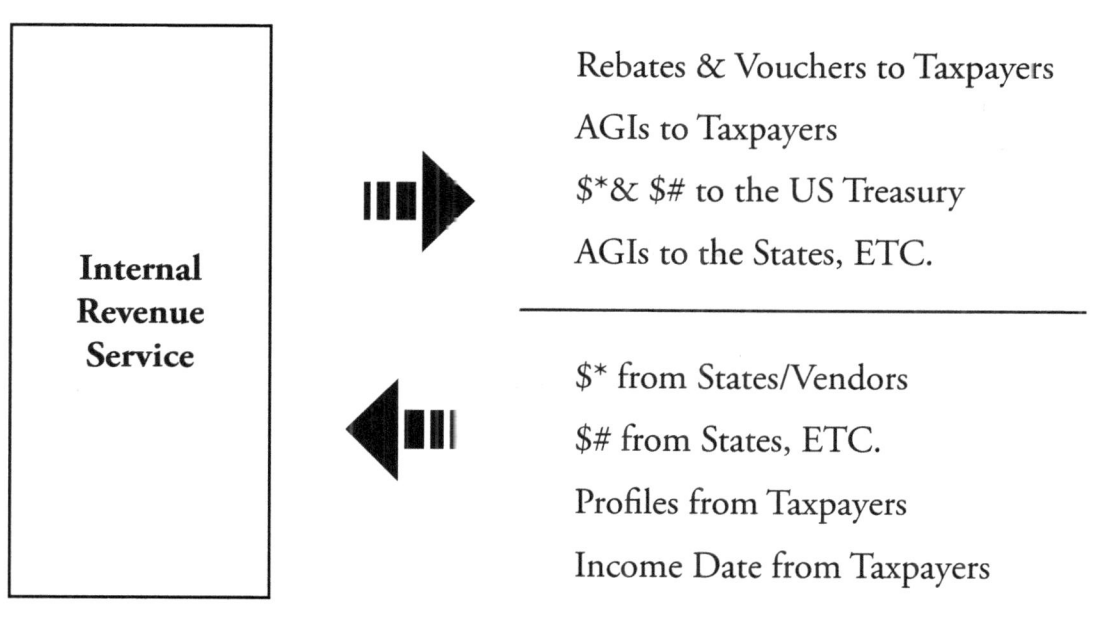

Figure 1-3 IRS – Principal Functions

A Bigger Role for the States

What will the states do and not do?

- The States **will** expand their revenue collecting agencies to collect the National Sales Tax.

- The States **will** collect Income Assessments Fes (just as they do now in collecting property value assessments).

- The States, Etc., **will** transfer National Sales Tax funds to the IRS on a monthly schedule.

- The States, Etc., **will** transfer Income Assessment Fee funds to the IRS on yearly schedule.

- The States, Etc., **will** establish a Tax Liaison Agency with the IRS to ensure compliance with The Simple Tax System (STS) law.

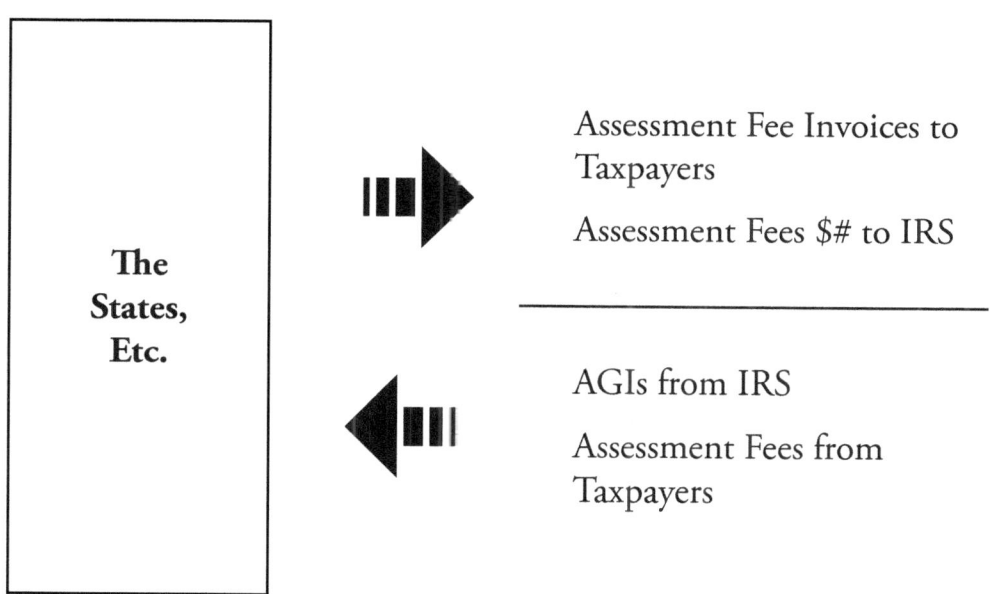

Figure 1-4 The States, Etc. – Principal Functions

What should Congress do and not do?

Will Congress make tax revenues fit the Budget or will Congress make the Budget fit the tax revenues?

Congress **will** have to adopt the framework of the Simple Tax System (STS) based on the concepts for a central National Sales tax, complemented with rebates for low-income learners and exemptions for Special people.

Congress **will** have to establish a yearly National Sales Tax rate.

Congress **will** have to establish percentage bracket amounts for disposable income, rebates and income assessment fees.

Congress **will** have to establish uniform exemptions for all categories of income earners.

Congress **will** have to complete the details of the Simple Tax System, Legislate and pass the bill and send it to the President for his signature prior to the 2024,2025,2026,...et.al., Christmas recess.

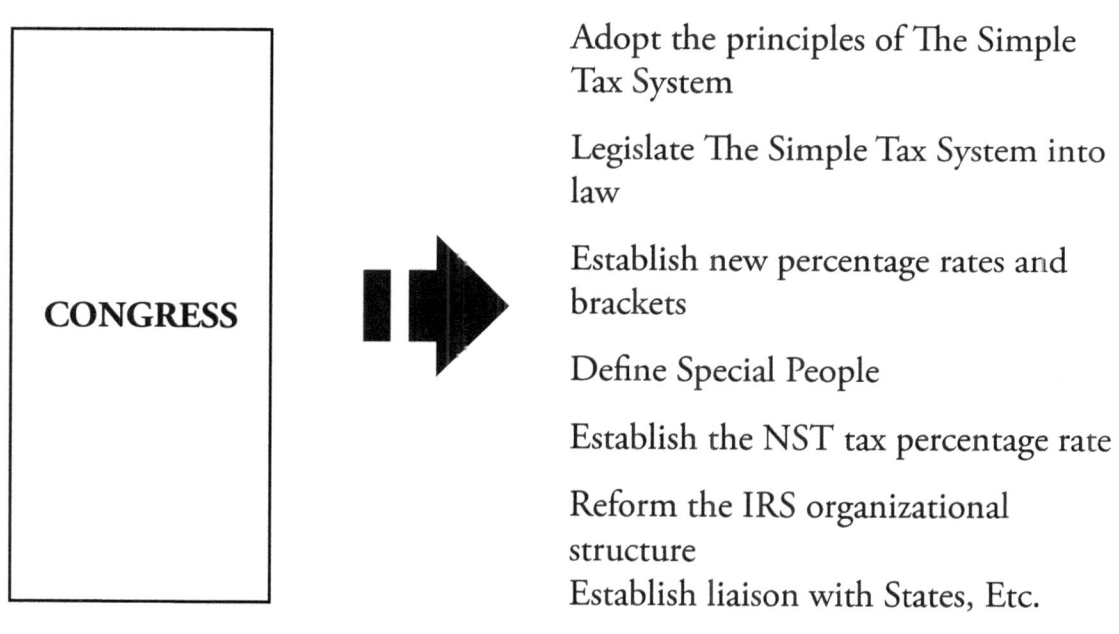

Figure 1-5 CONGRESS – Principal Functions

April 15 deadlines are no longer crucial.

A significant *less stressful role* for individuals,....

Taxpayers are required to report their income and profile if they want to request a TAX REBATE:

They **should** submit:

- All W2s, 11099s and other earning statements
- Documents that add income to other entities
- Dependents profiles
- Cost of doing business documents
- Legitimate contributions to charities

Note: if the taxpayer doesn't file, the IRS DOESN'T respond! That's the end of it, ... no harassment, fines, jail time, or other penalties.

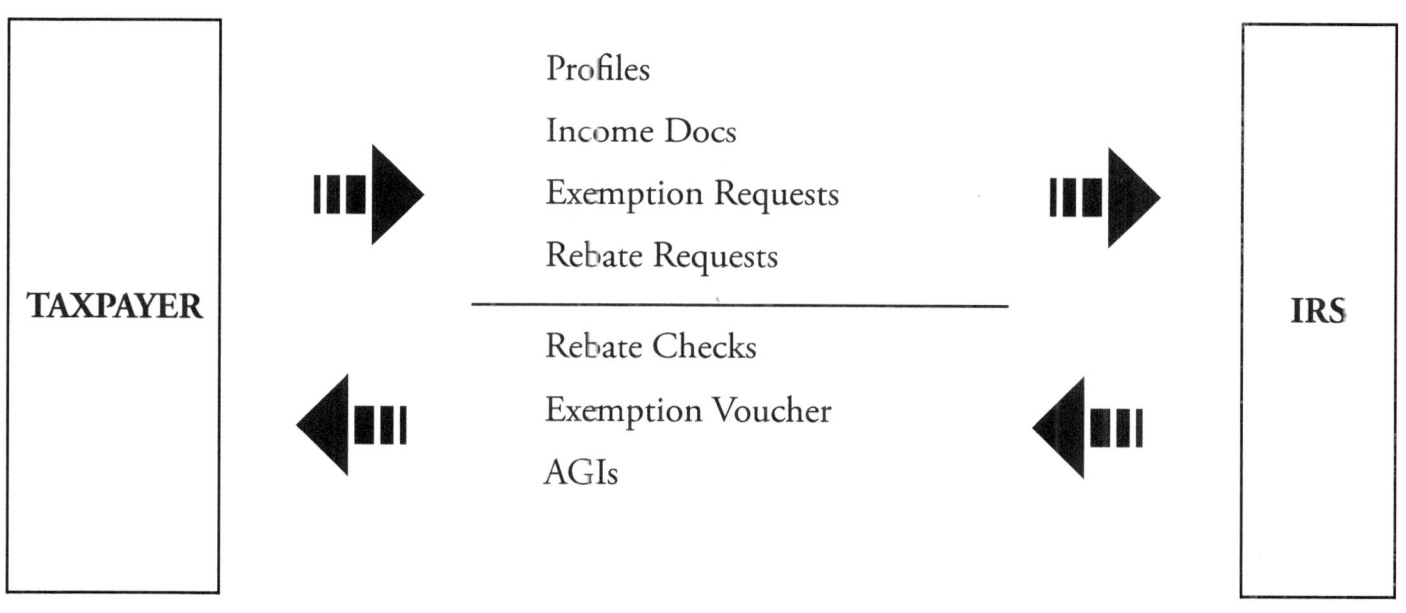

Figure 1-6 The Taxpayer – Principal Guidelines

A few words on ... Disposable Income

If you live from hand-to-mouth,...

If you live from paycheck to-paycheck, ...

If you're just keeping your head above water, ...

If there's too much month left at the end of your money, ... then

Your Disposal income is ZERO!

Note: Disposal Income Doesn't pay the bills, ... or even contribute to savings and investments.

The Simple Tax System and the Disposable Income Rebate

Absolute Truths:

After the bills are paid savings are deposited, what's left over is disposable income; money that does not have purpose.

Disposable income is affected by exemptions and deductions.

Disposable income normally increases tax receipts. Taxpayers with disposable income tend to buy things they consider as not essential.

DISPOSABLE INCOME BRACKETS

Less than 50K	20% of AGI Rebate
50K to 100K	15% of AGI Rebate
100K to 150K	10% of AGI Rebate
150 to ?	0% of AGI Rebate

A few words on ... Essential Income

If you live a comfortable lifestyle, ...

If your income is more than your output, ...

If you look forward to paying your bills, ...

If there's more money left at the end of the month, ... then

Your Essential Income is More than You Need

Essential Income pays the bills, contributes to savings and investments and adjusts upwards as you prosper.

The Simple Tax System and Essential Income

- Absolute Truths:

  Essential income is essential

  There is no such thing as too little or too much Essential Income

- Assumptions:

  1. Essential income is loosely tied to life-style and Cost of Living
  2. Essential; Income is firmly tied to jobs.
  3. Essential Income normally increases with prosperity.

Income Rebate Brackets

After taxpayer receive their AGI they can decide whether to apply for a rebate, ..., or not. The Income Rebate is calculated by applying the Bracket Rebate % amount to the amount of taxes paid. (Examples to follow)

AGI Brackets

LESS Than $25K	100%
$25K to $35K	40%
$35K to $50K	30%
$50K to $100K	20%
$100K to $150K	15%
$150K to $200K	5%

Note: AGI is adjusted gross income

Income Assessment Brackets

High income taxpayers will be assessed to fee on their income and a rebate (incentive) on a yearly increase in income. Assessments are administered by the State. (Example to follow)

Income Assessment and Rebate Brackets

$200K to $250K	1%
$250K to $1M	2%
$1M to $5M	4%
$5M to $10M	5%
More than $10M	10%

The States',... "A Bigger Role"!

The Simple Tax System (STS) will use existing tax agencies to collect the National Sales Tax and the Income Assessment fees.

- Forty-three States have agencies to collect the NST as a function of purchases made in their State, i.e., increase the State Sales tax rate to accommodate the addition of the National Sales Tax.

    (Note: The 7 delinquent states will be required to create the NST collection agency).

- All Fifty States have agencies that collect property taxes and property assessments. Therefore, these agencies will be mandated by Congress to collect income assessment fees on AGIs from high income earners who reside in their State.

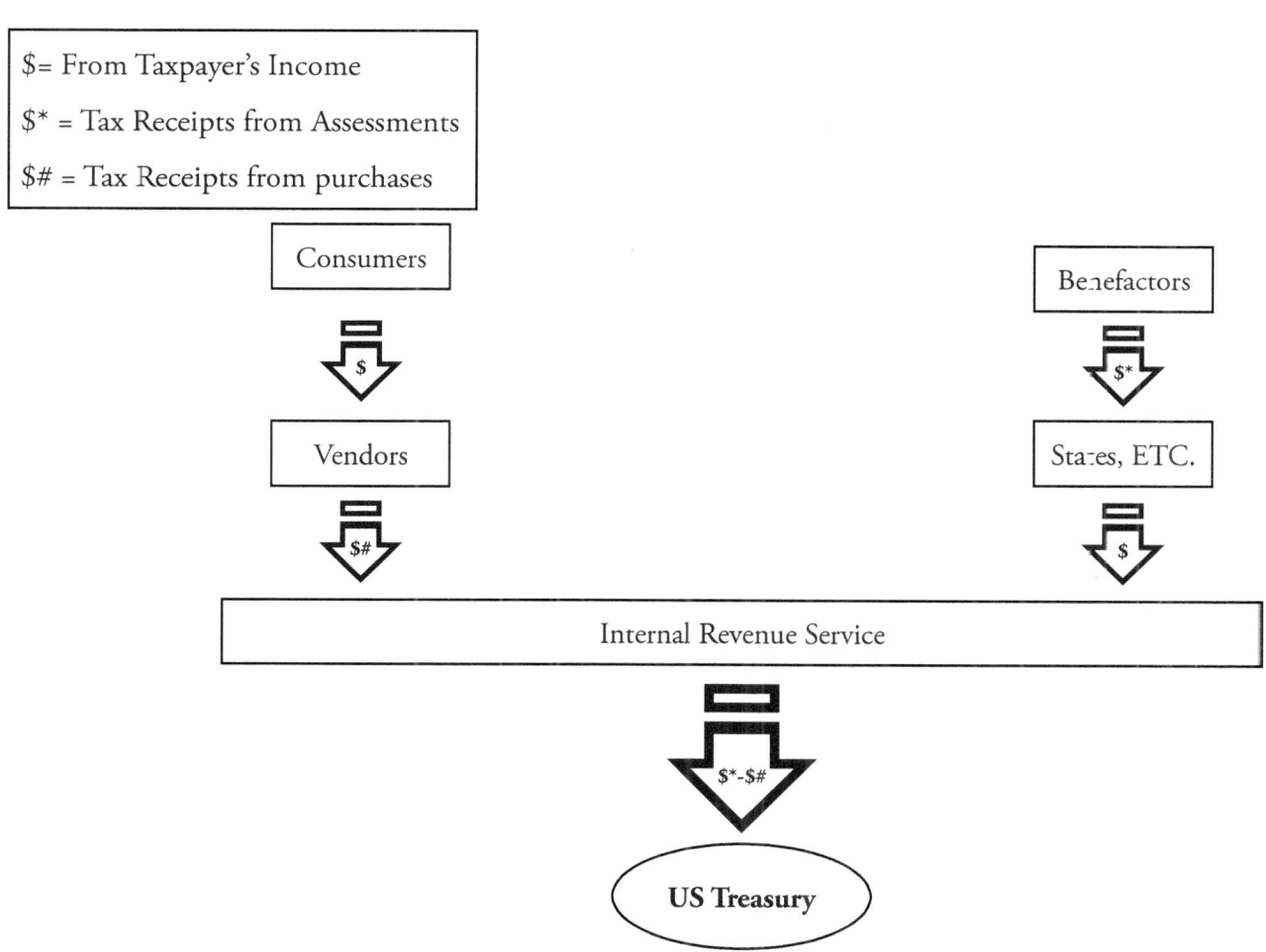

Figure 1-7 The Simple Tax System Money Flow

The *NEW IRS!* NOW!

Under the Simple Tax System framework, IRS' *POLICE POWERS* are dramatically reduced.

NO MORE: ...

INTIMIDATION,... .GARNISHING WAGES,... PROPERTY SEIZURE,...

TAX LIENS,... BANK LEVIES,... and, no more ...

Making Your Life MISERABLE!

The *NEW* IRS! In Transition

The *New* IRS will still be involved in the month-to-month transfer of funds to the US Treasury

They will also:

- Verify taxpayer's AGI against W2s, 1099s, etc., reported to the IRS. IRS taxpayer mitigation may be needed.
- Issues rebates to individuals who request rebates and issue exempts vouchers to <u>Special People</u>. These activities will quicky become routine.
- Collect National Sales Tax receipts from the States. These activities also will quickly become routine.

<u>Again: there is no longer a direct transfer of funds from taxpayers to the IRS</u>

The Simple Tax System – How does it work?

Rebate Example I for incomes below $200K

Adjusted Gross Income (AGI) - $40,000
AGI Rebate Bracket -   30% of NST
Disposal Income Rebate Bracket -   20% of AGI Rebate
NST paid = $40,000 @ 12.5% = $5,000
AGI Rebate   30% of $5,000 = $1,500
Disposable Income Rebate   20% of $1,500 = $300
TOTAL TAX paid = $5,000 minus $1,800 = $3,200

Tax Rate of 8.00%

This page is intentionally left blank

The Simple Tax System – How does it work?

Rebate Example II for incomes below $200K

Adjusted Gross Income (AGI) -	$60,000
AGI Rebate Bracket -	20% of NST
Disposal Income Rebate Bracket -	15% of AGI Rebate
National Sales Taxes paid =	$7,500
AGI Rebate 20% of $7,500 =	$1,500
Disposable Income Rebate	15% of $1,500 = $225
TOTAL TAX paid = $7,500 minus $1,725 =	$5,775

Tax Rate of 9.625%

This page is intentionally left blank

The Simple Tax System – How does it work?

Rebate Example III for incomes below $200K

Adjusted Gross Income (AGI) - $120,000
AGI Rebate Bracket -   15% of NST
Disposal Income Rebate Bracket -   10% of AGI
National Sales Taxes paid @ 12.5% $15,000
AGI Rebate   15% of $1,5000 = $2,250
Requested Disposable Income Rebate   10% of $2,250 = $225
TOTAL TAX paid = $15,000 minus $2,475 = $12,525

Adjusted Tax Rate of 10.437%

This page is intentionally left blank

The Simple Tax System – How does it work?

Rebate Example IV for incomes below $200K

Adjusted Gross Income (AGI) -	$225,000
AGI Rebate Bracket -	5% of NST
Disposal Income Rebate Bracket -	0% of AGI Rebate
National Sales Taxes paid @ 12.5%	$28,125
AGI Income Rebate -	5% of $28,125 = $1,406
Disposable Income Rebate	NONE
Income Assessment Fee @1% of AGI -	$2,250
TOTAL TAX paid = ($28,125 + $2,250) - $1,406 =	$28,969

Tax Rate of 12.875%

This page is intentionally left blank

The Simple Tax System – How does it work?

Rebate Example V for incomes below $200K

Adjusted Gross Income (AGI) -	$15,000,000
AGI Rebate Bracket -	0%
Disposal Income Rebate Bracket -	0% of AGI Rebate
National Sales Taxes paid @ 12.5%	$1,875
AGI Income Rebate -	0%
Disposable Income Rebate	NONE
Income Assessment Fee @10% of AGI -	$187,500
TOTAL TAX paid = $1,875K + $187.5K =	$2,062,500

Tax Rate of 13.75%

This page is intentionally left blank

A few thoughts about

EXEMPTIONS ...

- <u>Special People</u> are granted exemptions
- Exemptions are cash grants to the taxpayer
- Vouchers are issued to <u>Special People</u> to use as they want
- <u>Special People</u> are defined and approved by Congress

Special People ... Who are they?

- Veterans (weighted benefits; low to high): -

    Volunteers – 3+ years non-combat, combat/multi tours, combat wounded, combat disable, CMO recipients, POWs, CMO surviving spouse or next-of-kin (NOK).

- Homeland Contributors:

    Investors, researchers, philanthropists, Volunteers

- Care Givers:

    Moms, Dads, Legal Guardians, Volunteers

Note: CMO (Congressional Medal of Honor), POW (Prisoner of War). MOF (Medal of Freedom), NOK (Next-of-kin).

A few personal thoughts about ...

DEDUCTIONS ...

- Deductions will increase rebates by decreasing AGI
- Deductions will decrease assessments by decreasing AGI.
- Deduction for Mortgages, Charities and Child tax Credit appear to have bipartisan support in Congress now (2015)
- <u>*Deductions are evenly applied to all taxpayers.*</u>
- Only Congress determines what is deductible.
- Any authorized expense to the taxpayer's income that benefits the income of another taxpayer should be deductible, i.e., interest paid and CODB.
- The IRS considers authorized deductions when calculating the taxpayer's AGI

Note: Opinion: The Child Tax Credit should be granted to any taxpayer who is responsible for the care of another person, regardless of age and relationship to the taxpayer, care to include the same care given to a child

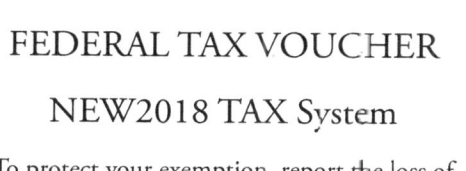

FRONT

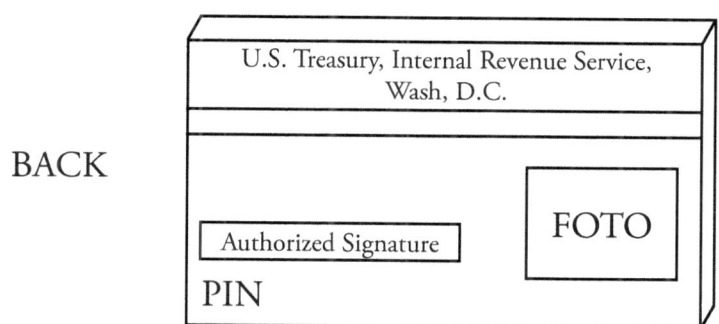

BACK

Figure 1-8 The Federal Tax Voucher for Exemptions and Rebates

What else ...?

- The Simple Tax System (STS) has to produce the same amount of FY budget funds that is produced now by the existing tax system.
- The National Sales Tax amount will be determined annually by the GAO and approved by Congress.
- Assessment fees from high income earners are meant to fund the Rebate systems and make up for the loss of revenue caused by exemptions and deductions.
- "Deductions" only include items which add income to the other taxpayers or other taxing authorities...

And, the will of Congress to implement these radical tax reforms."

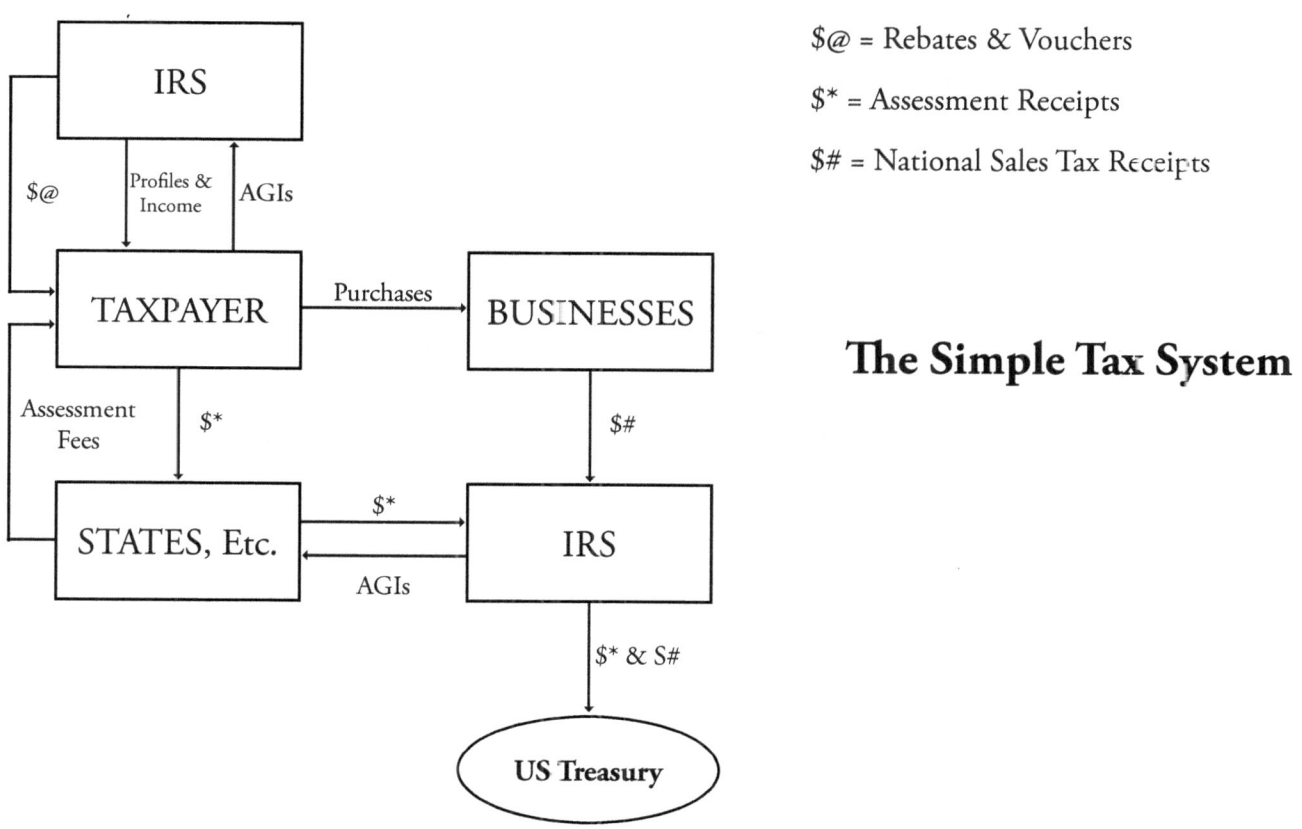

Figure 1-9 Information and Money Flow

The Simple Tax System

Concluding Remarks

- The Simple Tax System will give individual incentives to participate and incentives to prosper. It is a "Framework" for **RADICAL REFORM** OF THE US Tax Code. There Are features included to please Liberals, Conservatives and Moderates.

- The States, etc. will systematically take over all of the tasks involved in collecting taxes, thereby (over time), eliminating the IRS.

- The Federal Withholding Tax will be scraped in the first year as a monthly flow of money is a by-product of the National Sales Tax. The federal government will no longer *get free money from the public.*

- The Simple Tax System (STS) will negate the need for the current Corporate Tax policy is a big business will be treated the small as small business and individuals, generating tax dollars with purchases; big business will be treated as a consumers. Yes, there will be a consumer with the name of General Motors. GMM will generate tax receipts in the same way as does an individual. GM buys stuff too!

The Simple Tax System

Fine-tuning

- Every percentage amount and bracket range in this presentation are candidates for change.

- Delete, modify or keep Disposable Income Rebate, as well as any other rebate or fee herein described. The Income Rebate feature and the Assessment fee feature, however, are sacrosanct to the implementation of The Simple Tax System (STS).

- Special people could be expanded, deleted or further limited from the proposed exemption recommendations.

- Every assumption made by the author in this presentation may be considered nonsense and/or just sophomoric.

- The Simple Tax System (STS) will delete the federal withholding tax, quarterly payments and separate business taxes.

The Simple Tax System – About the Author

The author is a senior US citizen, concerned taxpayer; retired and now free to do nothing or something. As a novice author, this newbie feels it's time to express his opinion on tax reform in print media rather than in social conversation. He is an avid student of the U.S Constitution and the Federalists Papers. *

So, regardless of whether this presentation please you, bores you to tears or you dismiss is as utter nonsense, keep one thing in mind, ...,

It's only the author's opinion.

So, ... Snap out of it!

Note: *The Federalist's Papers, authored by Alexander Hamilton, James Madison Jr. and John Jay, were a compilation of essays supporting the Constitution.

Ramblings

Think about it, the great state of Florida has a 6% sales tax. Many other states have sales taxes too. How did this tax come about? Just how does each state gather these funds? And, to what end?

Yes, many states have a state-wide tax on goods and services. Everyone refers to this tax as a sales tax. In Florida most everything you buy has an additional 6% added to the total purchase price. These funds are transferred to the state's treasury on a scheduled basis.

Note: Just for chuckles ask your local small business owner/ manager how and when do they transfer the sales tax receipts to the state.

An important point to note here is that the funds are not transferred in advance of sales. So, the state is not looking for these funds in advance to pay for ongoing services which the state provides to its citizens. Why is that important? Because, in contrast, the federal government requires income tax funds from individuals to be paid in advance. A tax refund from the federal government is actually an interest free loan payback. So, if you enjoy giving your money to the government for a year without any strings attached, knock yourself out. Ignorance is bliss!

The contrast between state sales tax system and the federal government income tax system is startling - a real eye-opener. Let's ask ourselves a few questions.

Do you concern yourself (worry) about repercussions from authorities if you don't pay sales tax? I doubt if you even give it a passing thought.

Do you concern yourself (worry) about repercussions from authorities if you don't pay your income tax? Not yes but, HELL YES! You could have your wages garnished, your property seized or aliened, you could be arrested and sentenced to jail time and ordered to pay fines.

Is there a deadline or particular date in the calendar year when state sales taxes must be paid? No, state sales taxes are paid when you purchase something (goods or services).

There is a date deadline for paying federal income tax as well as state income tax. Miss the date and reap the consequences. Pay late and pay a penalty. Don't pay or just ignore and, Oh My!

Is it possible to pay state sales tax late and be subject to penalties? No.

Do you have to archive receipts from transactions that result from paying state sales tax? No. Only if you claim a deduction on your federal income tax return (current law). The federal income tax system requires that you archive several previous year's tax returns for possible audit by the Internal Revenue Service.

Do you need to enlist accountants and tax specialists to assist you when you pay state sales tax? No. There are no tax documents or related requirements.

Do you pay a higher percentage of state sales tax if you are a high-income earner and less if you are not as fortunate? No. There is no connection between your income and the percentage assigned to the state sales tax (but there could be- keep reading). However, there is a connection in the federal income tax system. higher earners paying a higher percentage.

The latest tax reform proposal consists of establishing three tax brackets (presently there are seven tax brackets) for individuals and lowering the corporate tax rate from 35% to 15%. On the surface, very attractive. But this proposal is not a new. innovative approach. It's what administrations past have done. There is nothing new here. It is merely a "fiddling" maneuver with the number of tax brackets and the percentage amounts associated with those brackets. A future administration will continue to fiddle, again changing the brackets and percentage amounts. And so, it will go on, and on. and on.

I am hopeful that at some point our leaders will recognize that the heart of the tax reform issue is the source of funds that are taxed. We continue to tax income and fiddle with the amounts taxpayers have to pay.

Let's stop taxing income and try something really new. Let's tax sales. Let's repeal and replace the individual and business tax system.

But we already tax sales, don't we? No, we don't tax sales at the federal level; only the state level in those states that have adopted a tax on sales.

So, what if we used commercial sales to provide funds to operate the federal government? What would change? First and foremost, the "federal sales tax system" would have to generate an amount to support the federal budget. In 2015, the federal government took in three trillion dollars in tax revenue from individuals and business. Unfortunately, the government spent four trillion dollars, creating a need to borrow one trillion more to pay the bills. Congress was too embarrassed to go back to the US taxpayer and ask them to fund the shortfall, instead they went money shopping on the international) ending market finding there a group of willing Shylock countries.

In any case, the federal government knows the worth of all the goods and services sold every year. They diligently track that data. It's not rocket science to calculate the percentage amount required to create three or four trillion dollars. If individuals and businesses create twelve trillion dollars in goods and services, then the tax on those sales would have to be 25% to generate three trillion or 33% to generate four trillion. How would you like to pay 33% more on everything you buy - even if the current income tax system was totally scraped? I wouldn't!

So, sticker shock is the problem. Again, however, repealing and replacing the income tax system with a national sales tax won't necessarily create a sticker shock percentage if the folks in the OMB and GAO scratch their collective heads and focus on generating the average and increasing and decreasing the tax on various categories, i.e., business purchases, individual purchases, big ticket purchases, luxury purchases, general purchases, essential purchases, etc. Perhaps then a reasonable target for a middle class tax amount could be settled at 10%.

The sales tax percentage could be varied much like the income brackets of the current income tax system. In Florida, middle class buyers would be required to pay $1.60 on a $10 essential purchase instead of $.60.

The Simple Tax System (STS) would be a permanent system much like the current system is permanent - requiring repeal legislation to get rid of it. The Simple Tax System (STS) framework would be permanent while the sales tax percentages could be manipulated to ensure that the individual taxpayer would pay just ten percent on essential purchases. Keep in mind ten percent will most likely NOT provide enough revenue to run the essential services provided by the federal government. Somewhere, someone will have to tighten their belts, somehow.

What other benefits would there be if the Simple Tax System (STS) were adopted?

First and most important the IRS will become toothless, no longer having a need to intimidate taxpayers with police powers and veil threats of incarceration, fines, liens and other penalties.

Another significant benefit is the elimination of the mountain of paperwork associated with the current income tax system. There is also no need to save any documentation concerning income unless the taxpayer wants to request a rebate or an adjustment in the income assessment.

DAMN THE U.S. TAX CODE

Even though legislative procrastination is the "rule of the day" in Washington, D.C., it seems inevitable that *We the People* will somehow, someday eventually convince Congress and the President to reform the present U.S. tax code. However, if our legislators and the President continue to dally, ... yes, *We the People* will revolt—a ground swell of discontentment not seen anytime recently for a political tax issue, a real kick'em all out tax revolt akin to the Boston Tea Party. It will happen, not if...but when.

Given, from time to time, Congress appears to agree that the national income tax system needs to be reformed. So, it is in 2017. What hampers Congress' initiative, however, is its inability to commit to radical change. Congress has a problem with "radical change" in anything. Radical change is frightening because radical change has historically been associated with unpleasant and sometimes violent actions from the people. The government believes they can continue to placate *We the People* by patching the current tax system, keeping the masses at bay, so to speak. After all, legislators have done that for decades. But patches on patches hastens the collapse of the item being patched. They don't seem to recognize that now, in 2017, *We the People* have had enough.

"Yes, indeed—we've had enough!"

REFORM

Lately there have been several alternative taxing ideas that have been introduced to the public by well-intentioned citizens, some politicians, and some just concerned individuals like me and the royal you. Figure 1-1 highlights a few of the most familiar.

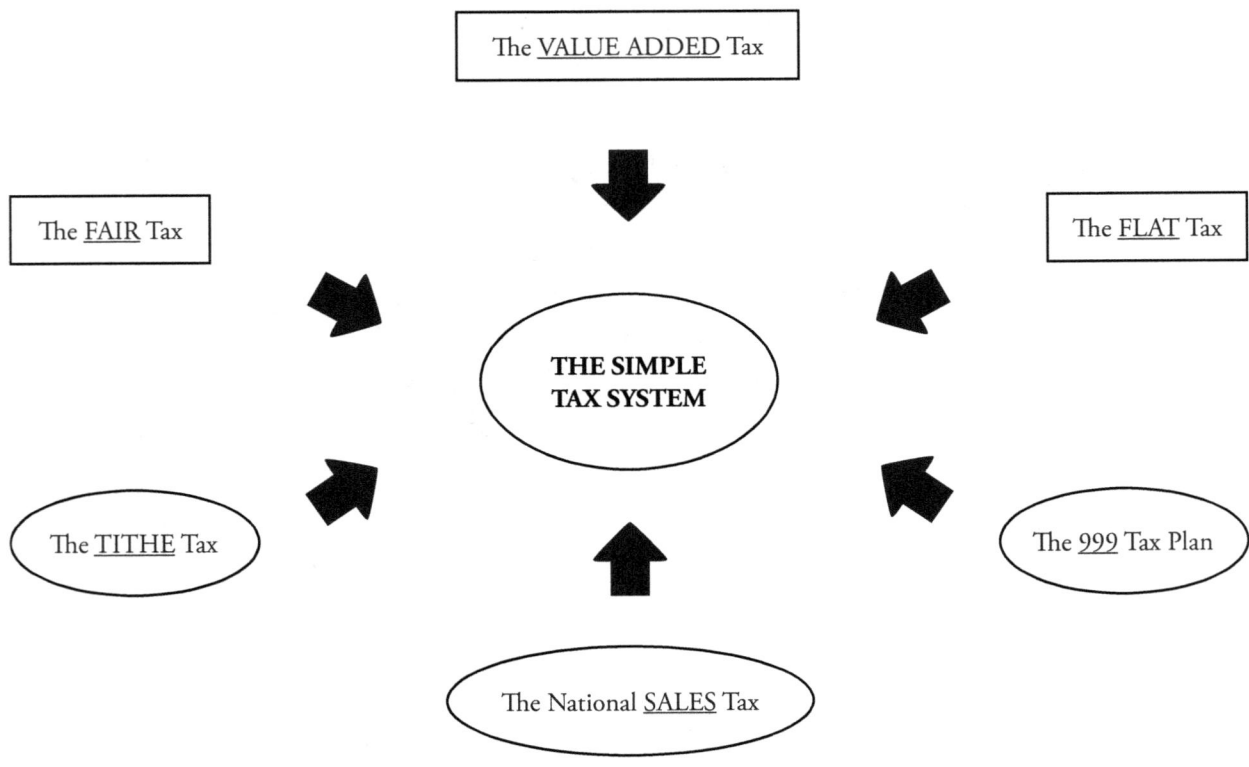

Figure 1-1 Alternative Tax Plans

We the People have embraced each one of these proposals with enthusiasm and cried out, "Go for it! Do it!" Our legislators. However, have preferred to pit each idea against the other, vying for bragging rights when one of the alternatives surges to the top as the favorite.

Consequently, nothing gets done-nothing but talk, nothing but hearings by as many committees as the legislators can muster. And. who is left waiting for something to happen? Yes, as always, *We the People*.

With a closer look at these so-called tax alternatives, one common element emerges. These proposals aren't radical at all. With the possibility of one or two features, they are merely meant to placate (again) *We the People*.

We the People want to throw the current tax system out, along with the K Street lobbyists and the IRS! Here's one man's opinion on the U.S. Tax Code:

> *"There is nothing fair about a tax code that is so complex that it is virtually impossible to comply with every aspect of the thousands of pages of rules and regulations. Because of the complexity of this code, the government can target virtually anyone and find a mistake in their tax documents, which can be used to extort money or worse. We are talking of nothing less than the precursor of a totalitarian government."*
> (Dr. Ben Carson - Washington Times, July 17, 2013)

Dr. Carson's preference for a tax code is based on biblical tithing, i.e., a flat tax on income. He dismisses the left's argument that it's not fair to the low-wage earner because it doesn't hurt the high wager as much. He counters: *"The problem with this line of reasoning is that no one can be completely objective determining exactly how much each person should be hurt."* (*Washington Times*. July 17, 2013)

Do you think the U.S. Congress would accept tax reform that incorporates a tithe (FLAT) tax?

The Simple Tax System (STS) herein proposed is centered around a FLAT tax but with one main difference. Funds (tax receipts) are not derived from income. Funds are derived from purchases. The central feature in The Simple Tax System (STS) is more like a Value Added Tax

(VAT) than the biblical flat tithe. Governor Mike Huckabee frequently refers to his main tax reform idea as a "Consumption Tax." His idea is a singular solution but far above any idea being offered by those who oppose radical change.

The Simple Tax System (STS) is a system. Think about the parts in your automobile that make it possible to move (go), to stop, and to change speeds. It would be impracticable to have an automobile with just a gas pedal and no brake pedal and transmission lever, or any combination that left one of these features out. You have to have some way to stop if you're moving and to move if you want to go someplace. Changing speed is also a necessary feature to make movement smooth and natural. The car's horn and windshield wipers don't have a role in this system.

The Simple Tax System is like the "Go, Stop, and Change Speed System" in your automobile. The Simple Tax System doesn't work without all of its essential parts-without its rebate feature, without its purchase feature, and without its high-income-earner assessment feature. Everything else is up for grabs.

On March 23, 2015, Senator Ted Cruz of Texas gave a speech at Liberty University. During the speech, the senator announced his intention to run for the office of President of the United States in 2016. Some have dubbed the speech "The Imagine Speech," as he asked the audience to imagine new circumstances in the future, presumably after he, Ted Cruz, became President. One of his imagine circumstances dealt with *imagine when you can file your taxes on a postcard*" (instead of the many pages now required under the U.S. Tax Code). The audience loved it and applauded vigorously at this suggestion. Well, when The Simple Tax System (STS) is adopted, the vast majority of taxpayers won't fill out a postcard sized return-they won't fill out a tax return at all, no postcard form, no forms, no hassle, no 15 April tax day!

Radical reform demands that our legislators adopt an "out of the box" approach. We've had enough dealing with income brackets, tax loopholes, and the endless confusion associated with the U.S. Tax Code's filing procedures. *We the People* need help. We don't understand the U.S. Tax Code. We're fearful of IRS reprisals and have endless worry about making mistakes. Will we be audited by the IRS? If so, can we support the audit? Do we have all of the supporting receipts, earning statements, proof of deductions? And can we afford the expense associated with filing our returns? Tax accountants can be budget busting. It's not getting easier to buy peace of mind.

Is there anyone willing to take on the IRS? We haven't found such a Don Quixote lately, but there have been a few in the past. Do *We the People* have a champion- a champion willing to stand up to the challenge? After all, the IRS can make your life miserable without recourse. They can be ruthless in their exchange with *We the People*, garnishing our wages, seizing our property, our fortune, and our future.

We the People are branded as tax cheats before we can defend ourselves.

What a lovely federal agency.

Because our government is the way it is, any tax reform has to be politically sensitive to our right-and left-leaning legislators- the same legislators who will be tasked to reform the Tax Code. If The Simple Tax System (STS) doesn't consider the ideology of the political landscape, failure is sure to follow. If both ideologies be damned, The Simple Tax System (STS) will be tossed on the scrapheap of tax reform alternatives, along with the others depicted in Figure 1-1. The Simple Tax System (STS) *MUST* contain features that will facilitate acceptance of opposite ideologies.

It is essential for The Simple Tax System (STS) to fit in, to take advantage of existing bureaucracies on the States, etc. (non-federal) level. Why do our legislators ignore the 10th Amendment? The 10th Amendment reaffirms that the States, etc., hold the key to tax reform. It's not breaking news-they always have.

So, what about the IRS? *We the People* are going to trash the IRS, correct? Well, yes, but not right away. Perhaps in a decade or so we'll be free of this behemoth agency, but not just yet now. You see, the royal YOU and the author really need the IRS to sign on, to fit in. So, let's just adjust their work direction, their short-term objectives, their mission. With a little help from the States, etc., *We the People* can do that.

We'll allow the IRS to focus, as they do now, on determining adjusted gross income (AGI) of individuals. That's what the IRS does now. They scrutinize the bejesus out of an individual's personal income, adding incomes from here and there and deducting expenses from hither and yon. Unfortunately, they are charged with collecting taxes on what they determine to be the outcome of that exercise. Not a good idea!

The Simple Tax System (STS) changes the character of the IRS- radically, but not immediately. For a while the income determination process is pretty much left as is. The IRS will continue to collect income documents and statements from employers and the individual as they do now. However, after the IRS (and the individual) mutually agree on the AGI. Both parties shake hands and walk away - for the time being, anyway. If and when they may meet again, it will be the result of the taxpayer's initiative - not the IRS'.

The Simple Tax System (STS) money machine (to fund the federal government) comes from a tax on the sales of good and services- a national sales tax. Everyone who buys something will pay this tax. They can reduce it, but they can't avoid it.

Figure 1-2 depicts the three essential features in The Simple Tax System (STS) the rebate feature, the assessment feature, and the national sales (consumption) tax feature.

After determining each taxpayer's AGI, the IRS and the taxpayer part ways. Further contact is not necessary. The taxpayer can update their income information on a yearly basis with the IRS - or opt out. But, if the taxpayer wants to reduce their tax burden, that they can do by requesting a rebate or applying for a partial refund on their income assessment. Lower-income earners can get a rebate. Higher-income earners can apply for a reduction on their income assessment if they continue to prosper. So, The Simple Tax System (STS) consists of the <u>National Sales Tax</u> (NST), the <u>Rebate</u> feature for lower-income earners, and the <u>Assessment</u> feature for higher-income earners. NST collections (from everyone) and Assessment Fees from wealthier taxpayers feed the government's coffers.

The rebate feature and the assessment feature are essential parts of The Simple Tax System (STS). Without them, this tax reform would simply be legislation that adopts a national sales tax. Such a reform would please the FLAT TAXERS but, knowing Congress' reluctance to change, they would merely adopt the national sales tax and retain the income tax system we now live under. The best of both worlds they would espouse. You sure?

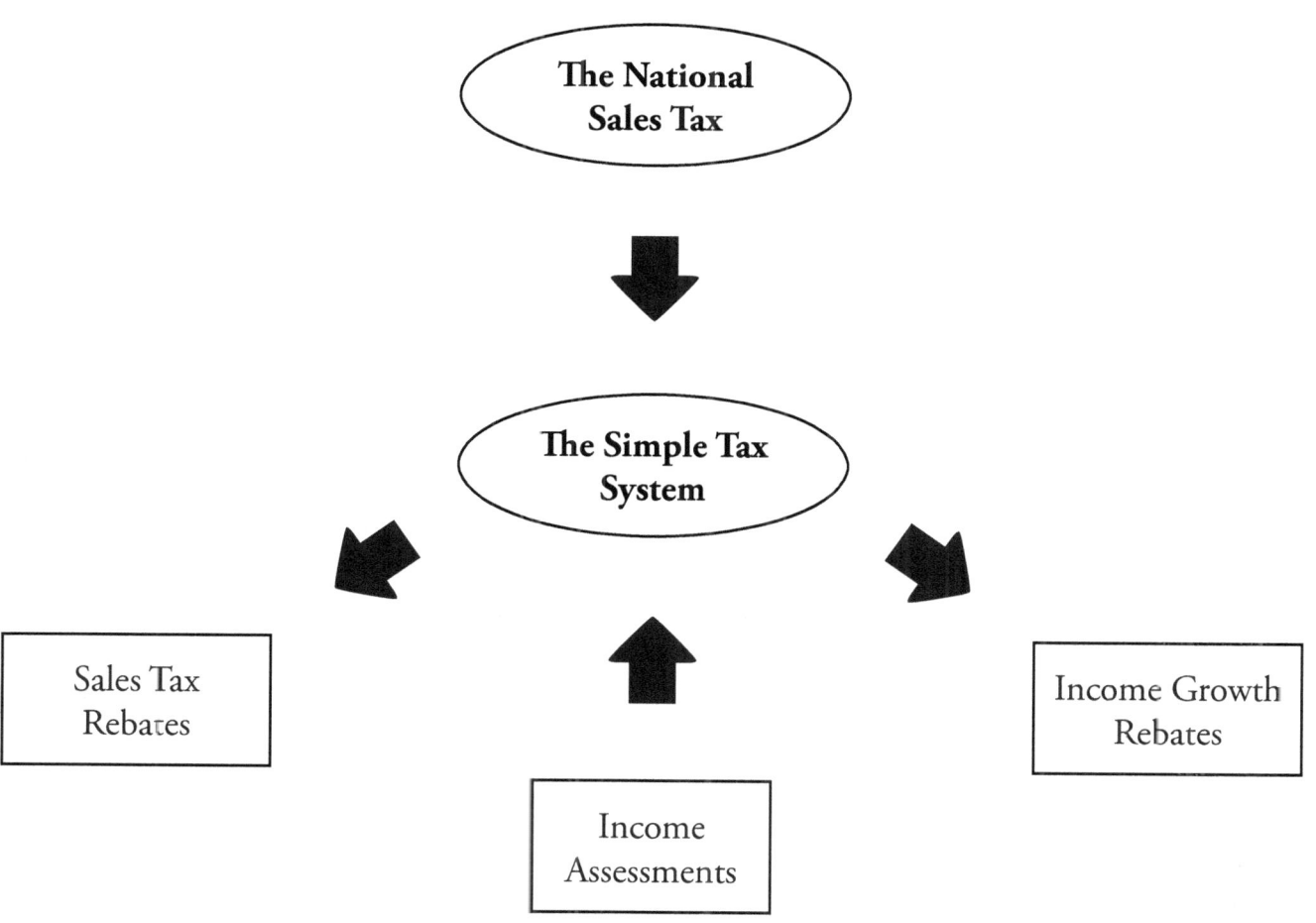

Figure 1-2 The Simple Tax System

How It Works

Every time someone buys something, taxes are collected. Under The Simple Tax System (STS), taxes will no longer be collected on a payday schedule (i.e., the Federal Withholding Tax), nor will taxes be collected quarterly from self-employed taxpayers. Under The Simple Tax System (STS), taxes will be collected by merchants and businesses on a daily basis, whenever they're open for business, whenever they engage in commerce with customers. Transfers of the NST funds can be made to the IRS electronically whenever they like and further passed on to the U.S. Treasury immediately.

The IRS will continue to be involved in determining AGI by matching employer-provided income information with that from other sources and the individual taxpayer. AGIs will be shared with the States, etc. The IRS will also collect individual profiles that will allow them to include authorized deductions in the AGI calculation. Taxpayer profiles contain the same information that is collected yearly under the current U.S. Tax Code. Under The Simple Tax System, the new taxpayers are the States, etc., and business vendors, not John and Jane Doe. Both the States, etc., and business vendors are historically accustomed to this responsibility. They do it now!

NOTE: The IRS forwards funds to the U.S. Treasury. It does not take funds directly from the taxpayer. It does, however, collect funds from the States and everyday vendors.

We the People have for far too long neglected the unique character of each State. *We the People* have for far too long neglected the mandate of the 10th Amendment to the U.S. Constitution.

The 10th Amendment to the U.S. Constitution states:

> *If all authority is not called out as a mandate of the federal government and the aforementioned authority is not called out as being prohibited in the States, then said authority belongs to the States or to the people.*

Holy cow! You mean to say that the Constitution forbids the federal government from dabbling in areas that are not included in the powers given to them in the Constitution (re: Article 1, Section 8)? Does that mean the federal government didn't have the power to tax individuals before the 16th Amendment was ratified? Boy! *We the People* are confused!

States have been the laboratories for many different legislative initiatives over the years.

The concepts of property taxes, school taxes, head taxes, and taxes on value are examples of authorities assumed by the States. The federal government used to keep its distance from these state and local initiatives, not infringing on them as the Constitution requires. The long-term goal of The Simple Tax System (STS) reform is to transition all of the IRS functions to the States in ten years.

In the interim, *We the People* believe the States can take over major IRS tasks by merely expanding the States' revenue collecting agencies. These agencies are operating efficiently on their own for their unique State's purpose. They only need to increase their tax rates and their assessment fees based on the income brackets depicted in The Simple Tax System (STS) presentation.

NOTE: The "States, etc." expression refers to the fifty U.S.A. states, the U.S.A.'s possessions, and the U.S.A.'s territories.

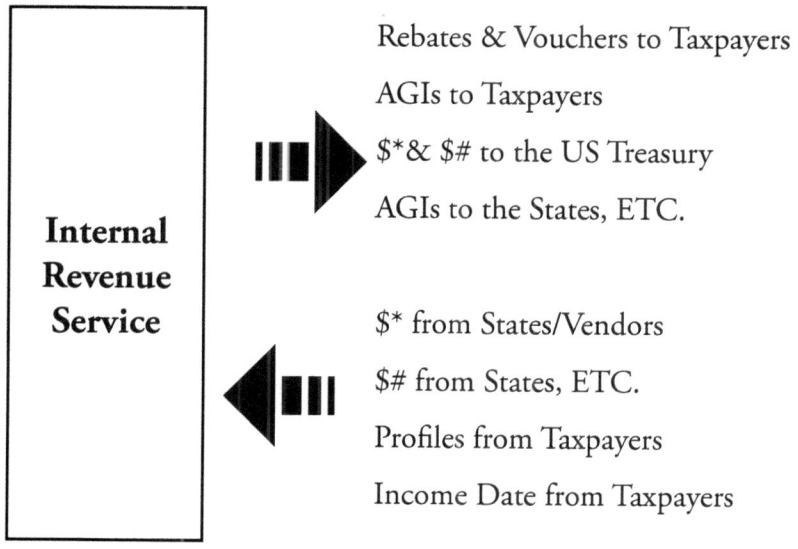

Figure 1-3 IRS — Principal Functions

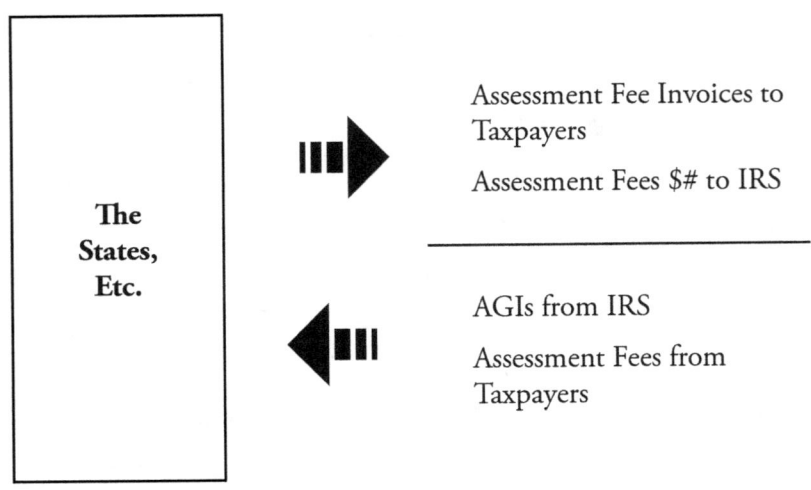

Figure 1-4 The States, Etc. – Principal Functions

Congress - A Player

So, what about Congress? What role will the honorable body play under The Simple Tax System (STS)? First and foremost, Congress has to adopt the concept and create the wherewithal to make it happen. Of course, there has to be a reconciliation between the amount of funds needed to run the functions of the federal government and the realities of increases and decreases as a result of the features of The Simple Tax System (STS). Congress will be tasked to do that within the restraint of a budget. When the word "budget" surfaces alongside "radical reform," Congress tends to return to a fetal position with thumb in cheek. Strong leadership is required to overcome this tendency.

As a consequence of knowing how much money is needed to run the federal government, Congress will have to resolve the percentage amount of the NST and the effect of offsets (plus and minus) that will result from the Rebate and Assessment features. This effort is not insignificant because bracket ranges for these features will be driven by their effect on the budget. Likewise, Congress will have to weigh the effect of defining special people, exemptions, and deductions.

Ho hum - stuff we hired them to do!

Getting back to getting started, Congress will also need to convince the President to sign whatever legislation they formulate to accommodate The Simple Tax System (STS). Such a task could undo the entire reform effort. It would be wise to promote this reform as the President's signature legacy legislation, relegating the Affordable Care Act and all the controversy surrounding it to the backburner.

When Congress accomplishes its mission and The Simple Tax System (STS) is law, then we can drop the asterisk and replace it with the teen year number. It has a chance on becoming The Simple Tax System (STS), however slim as that may be. Figure 1-5 depicts the principal functions of Congress.

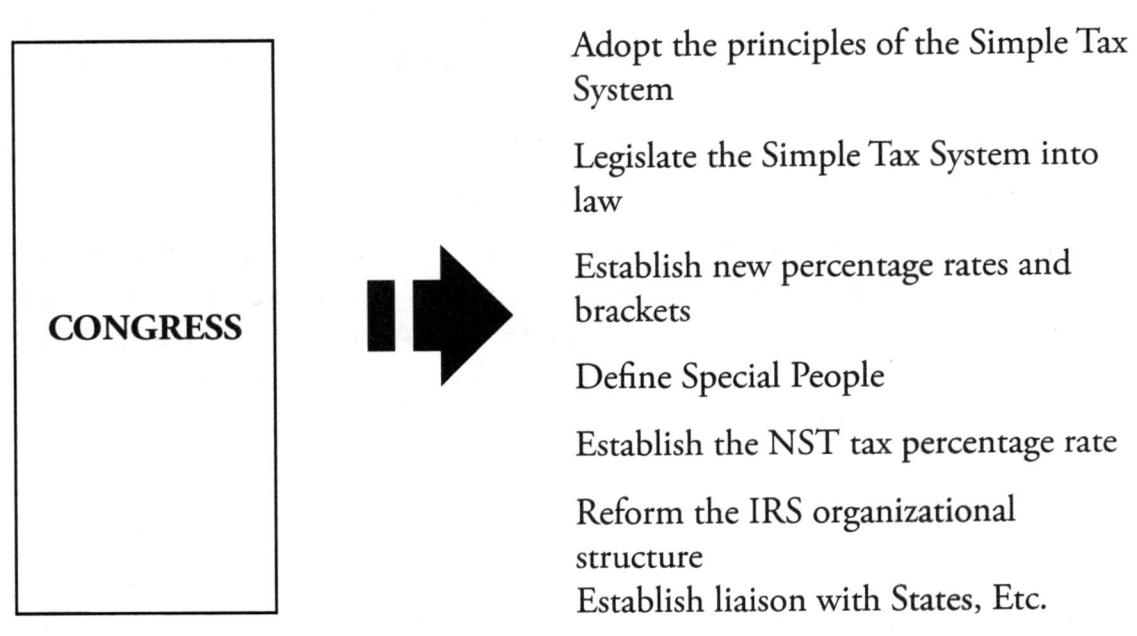

Figure 1-5 CONGRESS – Principal Functions

Consumers And Benefactors

Under The Simple Tax System (STS), we have to look at taxpayers as consumers and benefactors. Consumers are those of us who purchase goods and services, regardless of our income level, i.e., everyone with money to spend. The benefactor class of taxpayers are those who have benefitted from the capitalistic economic model to the extent that they are considered wealthy. The benefactors not only contribute to the funds generated by purchases, but they are additionally asked to contribute a prorated portion of their income to the general good. So, taxpayers may attain the status of being labeled as wealthy. And when that happens, the assessment feature of The Simple Tax System (STS) is activated.

If taxpayers don't want to take advantage of reducing their taxes, that's okay with the IRS. They won't have to calculate AGIs or engage in the rebate process either with consumers or benefactors. The taxpayer has to initiate the rebate process. If he/she wants a rebate, he/she has to request it. It's up to them.

Applying for a rebate begins with determining the AGI the IRS and the consumer collaborate on this effort. It is the taxpayer who initiates this activity by submitting income documents to the IRS. Congress can ultimately stipulate the type of documents to be submitted for review. The presentation suggests documents including earning statements (positive and negative), dependent profiles, and charitable contributions. The outcome is the IRS arriving at an AGI for the taxpayer.

Now, the taxpayer has all he/she needs to request a rebate. But it's still up to him/her to request it. Congress will most likely establish a time limit to request a rebate, after which exceeding the limit will cancel the rebate process.

Hardly a day goes by where I don't think about advantages of The Simple Tax System (STS). Yesterday morning I happened to reach into my clothes closet for a fresh Polo when I noticed three small file boxes sitting on the floor in the far-back corner. They were not readily visible, but I immediately remembered what they contained: tax documents from years past. Then, thinking about The Simple Tax System (STS) and the need for saving tax documents, I couldn't justify a reason to save them. Think about it. Do you save your sales tax receipts from general purchases you make from day to day? I don't! Why? Because sales tax receipts have nothing to do with justifying income.

April 15 deadlines are no longer valid-a far less stressful role for individuals, particularly if they don't request a rebate. There's no longer a need to find a resting place for last year's tax documents.

Figure 1-6 depicts the role of the taxpayer and the IRS. It illustrates what the taxpayer provides to the IRS and what the IRS provides to the taxpayer.

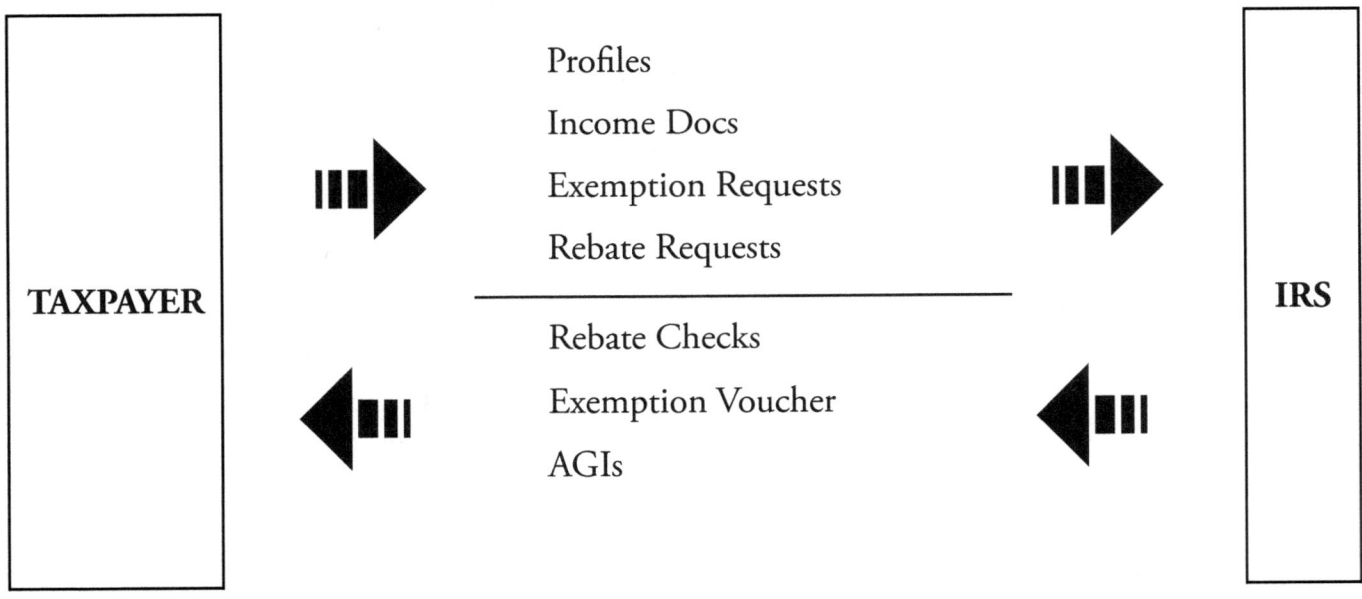

Figure 1-6 The Taxpayer – Principal Guidelines

Money for Nothing

Some say that Essential Income is what you need to live while Disposable Income is what you need to play. The presentation devotes several slides to explain the difference. The reason for this interlude of seemingly disconnected ideas is that The Simple Tax System (STS) makes an attempt to apply an additional rebate to lower- income earners based on the idea that there should be some kind of relief for earners who have little or no Disposable Income. Some may conclude that such a feature is not needed, only complicating The Simple Tax System (STS) framework and possibly hurting the acceptance of the tax system. Others, including the royal YOU, may conclude the opposite.

DISPOSABLE INCOME BRACKETS

1. Less than 50K = 20% of AGI Rebate
2. 50K to 100K = 15% of AGI Rebate
3. 100K to 150K = 10% of AGI Rebate
4. 150 to? = 0% of AGI Rebate

The presentation slides labeled "The Simple Tax System (STS) - How Does It Work?" show the tax calculations for several AGI amounts and the impact of the Disposable Income Rebate feature. AGIs above $150K are not eligible for the Disposable Income Rebate.

NOTE: I have assumed a NST of 12.5% for "The Simple TAX System - How Does It Work?" examples.

AGI REBATE BRACKETS

LESS Than $25K	100%
$25K to $35K	40%
$35K to $50K	30%
$50K to $100K	20%
$100K to $150K	15%
$150K to $200K	5%

NOTE: NO rebates on AGIs above $200K.

INCOME ASSESSMENT AND REBATE BRACKETS

LESS Than $25K	100%
$200K to $250K	1%
$250K to $1M	2%
$1M to $5M	4%
$5M to $10M	5%
More than $10M	10%

THE AUTHOR OUT OF CONTROL

Who do I think I am, creating rebate and assessment features, establishing income brackets and tax percentages and, yes, having the chutzpah to think The Simple Tax System (STS) is the answer to tax reform? I have simply developed a framework for tax reform. I don't view The Simple Tax System (STS) as the answer to tax reform. My view on The Simple Tax System (STS) is yet another alternative that possesses the radical reforms that have to be made to ensure the taxpayer's freedom from tyrannical actions of the federal government.

Who would object to a tax system that doesn't require a multitude of forms and documents to be submitted to the IRS every year; doesn't have a requirement to archive copies of those forms and documents for years to come; doesn't have a need to take a portion of your paycheck automatically every payday; doesn't threaten and intimidate you with reprisals, innuendos, and simple bullying; and yet encourages every citizen to participate in the process, even helping them to apply for refunds, never demanding more than what has already been collected?

Sounds pretty good, huh?

In addition to the rebate features, The Simple Tax System (STS) also contains an assessment fee, which is levied against high-income earners who have AGIs above $200k. Uh-oh! This sounds like "taxing income." Well, it is! The Assessment Fee feature does resemble the current income tax. The reason it is included in The Simple Tax System (STS) is to simply ask the wealthy to help offset the loss of funds as a result of the rebate features. It's really not a problem since the wealthy are clamoring to contribute more anyway. However, if the wealthy continue to prosper from year to year, they too can apply for a capital gain rebate based on the increase in their AGI

So, reporting AGI is more demanding for the high-income earner, but not necessarily, since the wealthy (and all property owners) are already paying property taxes on their residences. The Assessment Fee applied to AGIs above $200k begins at 1% and tops out at 10% for AGIs above $10M. The novelty associated with the Assessment Fee feature is that it is collected by the same state agencies that collect property taxes or state income taxes. Establishing AGIs are a necessity for higher income earners. They have to reconcile their AGI with the IRS every year. Could this be contentious? Not anymore, so then it is under the current income tax system. The IRS and the individual are merely agreeing on an AGI number that the state can use to apply the assessment fee. The assessment fees collected by the state are transferred to the IRS.

It's not important how the states collect the Assessment Fees. They are free to use whichever agency they feel is the best to get the job done. The states that have income tax agencies will probably want to use them. However, some states don't have income tax agencies, Florida being one. Florida may opt to use the property tax collecting agencies. It's up to the state to decide which one to use.

We've already discussed the 10th Amendment and the role of the States. Simply said and repeated again, the 10th Amendment tells the federal government (Congress) to "mind its own business", as described under its authorities listed in Article I, Section 8. Unfortunately, Article I, Section 8 contains the statement:

"... and provide for the common Defense and *general Welfare* of the United States "

The three words "and general 'Welfare" have opened the floodgate for federal spending.

Congress has stretched the expression "...*provide for the...general Welfare*" to include everything from national healthcare for illegal immigrants to cleaning your dog's teeth. Of course, these goodies come with an associated cost. There is no free lunch. and you have to pay the vet!

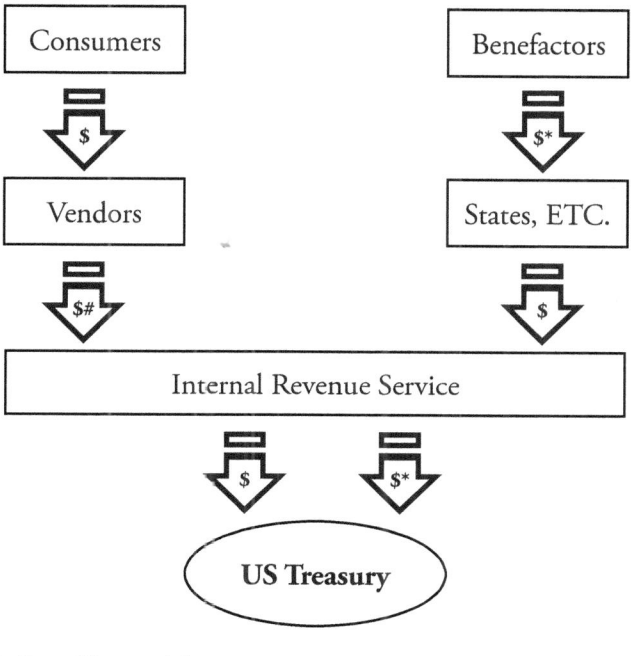

$ = From Taxpayer's Income
$* = Tax Receipts from Assessments
$# = Tax Receipts from purchases

Figure 1-7 The Simple Tax System Money Flow

Figure 1-7 depicts the information and money flow that's unique to the NEW201* TAX System. Note that there are Three sources of money:

1. S = private money owned by the taxpaying consumer,
2. S# = funds genera ted by the taxpaying consumer from everyday purchases of goods and services and passed on to the IRS by the sellers, and
3. S* = Assessment Fees levied against high-income earners.

What's missing from this figure is the outflow of money from the IRS in the form of rebates. So, while the IRS is forwarding tax receipts to the U.S. Treasury, it is likewise returning money to taxpayers. The outflow is not shown in the figure because it

is a process that has to be initiated by the taxpayer. If the taxpayer doesn't want to request a rebate, the IRS couldn't care less. No action on the part of the taxpayer results in no action by the IRS.

The new IRS will look a lot different than it does today. It will no longer be the menacing giant most of us fear. No longer will we be harassed, bullied, and threatened because there is no need for repressive tactics to force citizens to pay taxes. Buy something in the jurisdiction of the United States, and you pay taxes. They are no longer "your taxes." They're just taxes.

I live in Florida. There is no state income tax there, but there is a state sales tax. Under The Simple Tax System (STS), the governor of Florida will instruct the legislature to add a NST piggyback tax onto the state sales tax. Collection agencies will operate as they do now, going about their daily routine of collecting and distributing funds to the state government with the necessary deviation to send a daily transfer of NST funds to the IRS.

The governor will also instruct the state's County Commissioners to implement an additional assessment fee on each citizen's AGI if it exceeds the _"you're now classified as wealthy"_ limit set by Congress (recommended to be 1% on an AGI greater than $200K).

Good People and Questions

What about exemptions, deductions, child-tax credits, marriage penalties, etc.? Perhaps we can agree that there are "special people" who contribute to our national interests, who are worthy of some consideration. In particular, those who serve in our military should receive a stipend of some kind, graduated in amount and time for their contribution. Why shouldn't the federal government pay for services rendered to the federal government? If a person or family adopts a needy individual, providing care and essential services to them, doesn't that charitable action deserve consideration by the federal government for some kind of benefit? Doesn't this charity save money and resources that the federal government would have to provide? Doesn't this example depict a loss of income from the giver and an increase in income to the receiver?

Shouldn't our heroes who are awarded medals of valor receive a gratuity from the nation? Congress can decide who. Congress can decide what the gratuity should be. I have made some suggestions in the presentation. The IRS can issue vouchers or other plastic vehicles, much like store credit cards. (Figure 1-8 shows an example of a credit card of present-day technology. Such a device can be loaded with funds and securely discarded when the funds are exhausted.)

When an individual pays interest to a payer, that's income to the payer and a loss of income to the payee. Does the category of the interest payment matter? Why is interest on goods and services treated differently than interest on a mortgage? *We the People* don't get it. So, goes the U.S. Tax Code. Congress has to incorporate the principle of fairness in treating its citizens for deductions and exemptions. Can they do that?

Let's defer to Congress for these perks. There is little we can do about the K St. lobby anyway.

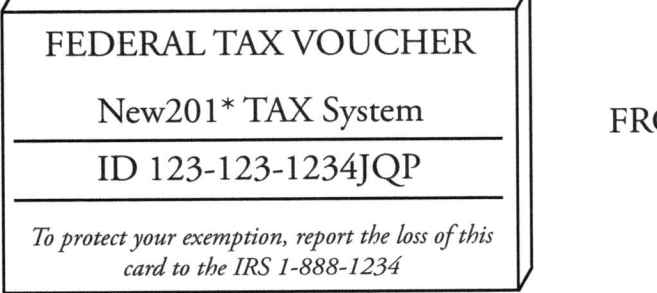
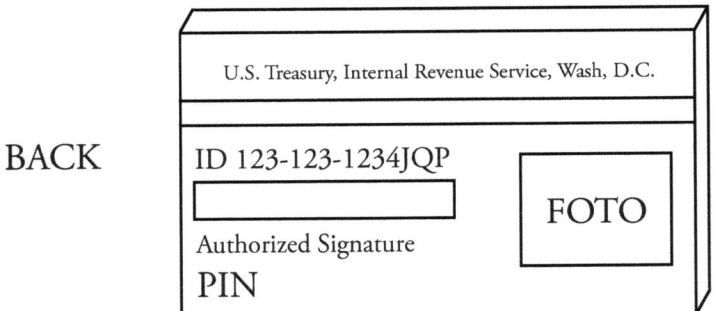

Figure 1-8 The Federal Tax Voucher for (credit card) Example

ALL FOR ONE... ONE FOR ALL.

The Simple Tax System treats individuals and business the same. With this approach, there is no longer a need to have directed business taxes. All businesses have an AGI just like *We the People*. Granted, most business AGIs will fall into assessment fee brackets. That's good! Wealthy businesses and wealthy individuals pay the majority of taxes anyway. Plus, if wealth grows from year to year, wealthy businesses and individuals are eligible for prosperity rebates. But if wealth diminishes, so does the assessment fees. We don't kick a taxpayer when he/she's down.

If your AGI is small or maybe zero, you are still eligible for rebates, exemptions, and deductions. Perhaps you're the unemployed wife of a wealthy man or, better yet, the unemployed husband of a wealthy woman. General Motors has an AGI just like every employee of GM, just like the unemployed wife and the unemployed husband. Just wait 'til next year.

"The Simple Tax System (STS) - How Does It Work?" examples show how funds are collected from taxpayers (or enterprises) with varying AGIs. For these examples, I have selected an NST of 12.5%. Is that too much or not enough? Don't know, don't care. Congress will have to determine the NST rate based on the amount of funds needed to run the agencies and bureaucracies of the federal government. The national budget is not addressed herein, nor is it intended to be addressed.

These examples show a tax burden that increases with higher AGIs. The examples depict a tax rate of 8% for an AGI of $40,000 and 13.75% for an AGI of $15,000,000. Remember, under The Simple Tax System (STS) we are not tied to income tax brackets because we are not taxing income.

The 16th Amendment to the U.S. Constitution (ratified February 3, 1913) states: *"The Congress shall have power to lay and collect taxes on incomes, from whatever source derived, without apportionment among the several states and without regard to any census or enumeration."*

Some have suggested that the 16th Amendment should be repealed. One could argue that the amendment only gives Congress credibility, much as does Article I, Section 8.

Why did Congress choose to tax income? Because they could. Didn't we already discuss this?

For exemptions, deductions, and special people, it's all about establishing an AGI that all can agree to. Of course, agreement has to backed by facts and physical evidence, hence the continuing need of the IRS. Remember, in The Simple Tax System (STS) if you can't agree on an AGI, that's okay. It just means that you have to defer your application for a rebate. If you don't care about getting a rebate or just give up on the AGI negotiation, that's okay, too. You either have a dog in this hunt or you don't.

Dollars and Sense

Figure 1-9 depicts the flow of money and information between the IRS, the taxpayer, businesses, the states, etc. It's not hard to follow, so I am deferring to your intellect. Frankly, I'm a bit weary of this conversation.

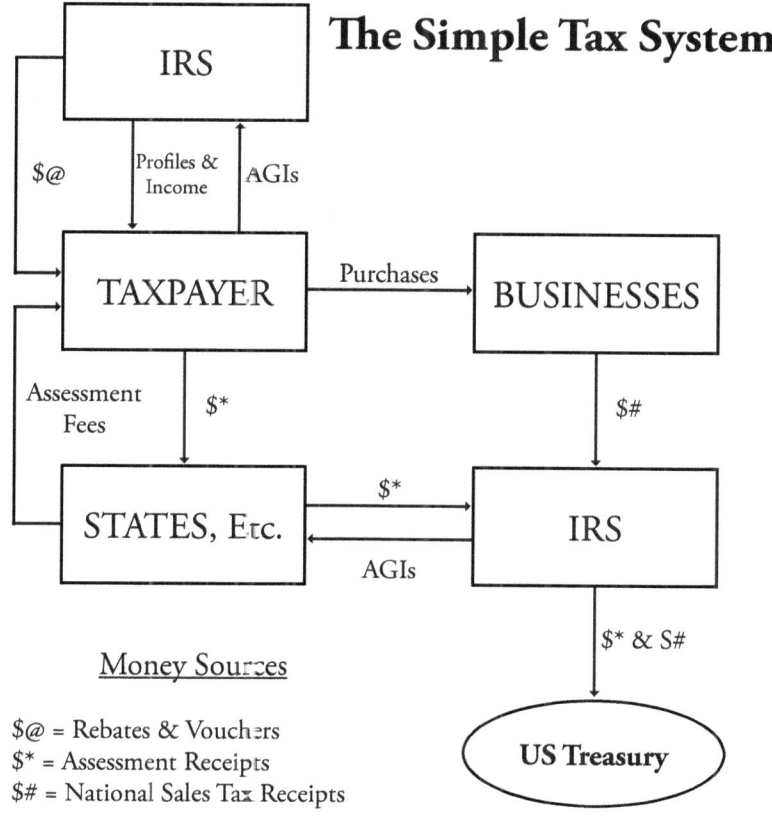

Figure 1-9 Information and Money Flow

And...?

Where do we go from here?

The future outlook for The Simple Tax System (STS) is not very good, solely because it's a radical change. The federal government does not like change- it never has. But, if adopted in some form that this framework provides, the nation will prosper beyond the most optimistic views-just one man's opinion. This change is something *We the People* want. Perhaps not in the framework of what we have proposed but maintaining the three-pronged principle of something for the left. something for the right, and something for the middle. As previously stressed, those three initiatives are sacrosanct.

One thinks we need to get exposure for The Simple Tax System (STS) through appealing to prominent politicians and seeking their sponsorship. The author tends to agree; however, he feels that the "not invented here" mentality of most politicians will result in certain death for the Simple Tax System (STS). Politicians and talking heads will tend to overlook the framework concept, assign it to policy status, and then just tear it apart- in public, of course.

Can we expect less?

www.ingramcontent.com/pod-product-compliance
Lightning Source LLC
Chambersburg PA
CBHW080525030426
42337CB00023B/4632